Somerset County
Pennsylvania

Somerset County
Pennsylvania

A History in Images

Sister Anne Frances Pulling, RSM, MS

THE
History
PRESS

Published by The History Press
Charleston, SC 29403
www.historypress.net

Copyright © 2007 by Sr. Anne Frances Pulling
All rights reserved

Cover image: A view of the Lincoln Highway, which crosses through five Pennsylvania counties.

First published 2007

Manufactured in the United States

ISBN 978.1.59629.240.6

Library of Congress Cataloging-in-Publication Data

Pulling, Anne Frances.
Somerset County, Pennsylvania : a history in images / Anne Frances
Pulling.
p. cm.
ISBN 978-1-59629-240-6 (alk. paper)
1. Somerset County (Pa.)--History--Pictorial works. 2. Somerset County
(Pa.)--History, Local--Pictorial works. 3. Somerset County
(Pa.)--Biography--Pictorial works. 4. City and town
life--Pennsylvania--Somerset County--Pictorial works. 5. Somerset County
(Pa.)--Social life and customs--Pictorial works. I. Title.
F157.S6P85 2007
974.8'79--dc22
2007003264

Notice: The information in this book is true and complete to the best of our knowledge. It is offered without guarantee on the part of the author or The History Press. The author and The History Press disclaim all liability in connection with the use of this book.

All rights reserved. No part of this book may be reproduced or transmitted in any form whatsoever without prior written permission from the publisher except in the case of brief quotations embodied in critical articles and reviews.

Contents

	Acknowledgements	7
	Introduction	9
1	Roof Garden of Pennsylvania	13
2	Jewels in the Mountains	27
3	Conemaugh	41
4	Land of Sweet Maple	61
5	Curiosities and Resorts	79
6	Berlin in America	97
7	Shanksville	113

Acknowledgements

This publication is based on research, records, periodicals, documents, newspapers and interviews with residents, many of whom graciously supplied information and offered constructive suggestions. A special thank you goes to Paul Pritts of Berlin; Robert Johnson and David Fox of Stoystown; and Betty Arnold and Marlene Nagle of Rockwood for sharing many photographs and a wealth of knowledge.

Gratitude is extended to Jim Oliver of the *Daily American* newspaper, Ben Vinzani of the Somerset Borough, Therese Marfario of Jennerstown, Squire and Phyllis Ickes of Boswell, Christopher Barkley of Windber, Cynthia Mason of the Meyersdale Public Library, T. Henry Cook of the Somerset Trust Co. and Bob Duppstat of Seven Springs Resort.

A prayerful gratitude goes to all who assisted in any way by supplying photographs, constructive suggestions and proofreading. I am especially grateful to my own religious community, the Sisters of Mercy of the Mid-Atlantic Community, for their support and encouragement in this project.

Introduction

Somerset County, in the Laurel Highlands of western Pennsylvania, presents a magnificent panorama to the traveler. Nature has lavished its bounty on this "Roof Garden of Pennsylvania." In the words of a founding father, "Nothing could exceed these plains in beauty." Somerset lies on a tableland, or plateau, between the Allegheny Mountains to the east, Laurel Mountains to the west, the Mason-Dixon line to the south and Cambria County to the north.

Mining iron ore and coal, farming and lumbering drew pioneers to the area, and by 1760 Somerset had become a prominent village. Harmond Husband was one of the area's earliest inhabitants. He was a Quaker who sought refuge in the Laurel Highlands from North Carolina, where he had helped form an opposition group known as the Regulars. They opposed the British government, which was imposing unfair taxes and fees. In 1769 the Regulars staged the very first armed resistance by colonists against the British on this continent. It was known as the battle of Alamance. The British were better armed and Husband, realizing defeat, fled to the northwest. He brought his family and settled in what is now Somerset. In 1774 the first plans were laid out for "Brunerstown," named by Ulrich Bruner, Peter Ankeny and Harmond Husband. This village later became known as Somerset.

Husband, who called himself the "Old Quaker," found himself in the midst of another rebellion in 1791 when Congress imposed a tax on whiskey. Distilling whiskey from grain was a common practice in the colonies, and in protest of the tax, Harmond Husband, along with General Robert Philson of Berlin, erected a liberty pole in the Brunerstown Square. They were arrested and sentenced to prison in Philadelphia. After one year in prison, at age seventy, the Old Quaker died of fever.

Over the years, Somerset, along with the rest of the country, witnessed the rise of faster and more extensive travel. The influx of automobiles created a need for adequate roads and in 1913, interested businessmen, led by Henry Joy and Carl Graham Fisher, formed the Lincoln Highway Association (LHA) and spearheaded the creation of a publicly funded road that would stretch across the country.

Introduction

Rural roads were not conducive to the new mechanical innovation that swept the country, and the Lincoln Highway was intended to stretch from New York to San Francisco over the shortest route practical. It was rugged yet scenic, rough yet attractive and harsh yet charming. This historic trail winds its way through the heart of Pennsylvania.

Gradually, attention-seeking entrepreneurs began lining the Lincoln Highway with attractive curiosities. The unique hotel and restaurant "Ship of the Alleghenies" was built on a Lincoln Highway mountainside in such fashion to give the effect of sailing on the ocean. The historic ship rode the mountain in Schellensburg for seven decades. In October 2001, when the hotel was consumed in flames, a stream of mourners gathered to pay their final respects. Former employees of the historic ship remembered it fondly with nostalgic affection. The Lincoln Highway Heritage Corridor plans to revive the ship in a twelve-foot, two-dimensional replica at the site.

Captivating as it was the Lincoln Highway was not conducive to speed. By 1940 part of the Pennsylvania Turnpike followed the proposed route of an abandoned railroad through the county. This required cutting through the mountains and creating the tunnels of today. The turnpike gave the motoring business the speed it hoped for.

Surrounding the metropolis of Somerset are numerous small and thriving entities, each of which retains a bit of nostalgia for a bygone time. A wide variety of denominations have their houses of worship in the area and church steeples pierce the sky above the trees.

Berlin is a prosperous little hamlet that houses Snyder's Potato Chip Manufacturing Company. The origins of this company date back to the original potato chip created at the Grand Union Hotel in Saratoga Springs, New York. The towns of Meyersdale and Rockwood became prominent for the maple products they harvest each year.

The town of Garrett in Somerset County boasts the state's first utility-scale wind farm. The first of its kind in the country, the wind farm was created in 2000 on a reclaimed strip mine above Garrett and features eight turbines sent from Denmark. Other similar farms around the state have since been developed. The windmills in Garrett are monitored from computers. The mill senses wind changes and automatically makes the necessary adjustments.

Tucked away in a fold of the Allegheny Mountains the tiny settlement of Shanksville, in Stonycreek Township, was home to undisturbed wildlife, a few strip mines and winter snows for several centuries. It was inhabited by two hundred friendly folks, and everyone knew everyone else—it had always been that way. It was here, in this quiet mountain retreat, on September 11, 2001, a deafening explosion shook doors and windows throughout the town, and a plume of smoke billowed high into the heavens, obscuring the brilliant autumn sky.

The quiet, rustic settlement was abruptly thrust into the national spotlight. Terrorism transformed the friendly little hamlet into a unique cemetery, a national

INTRODUCTION

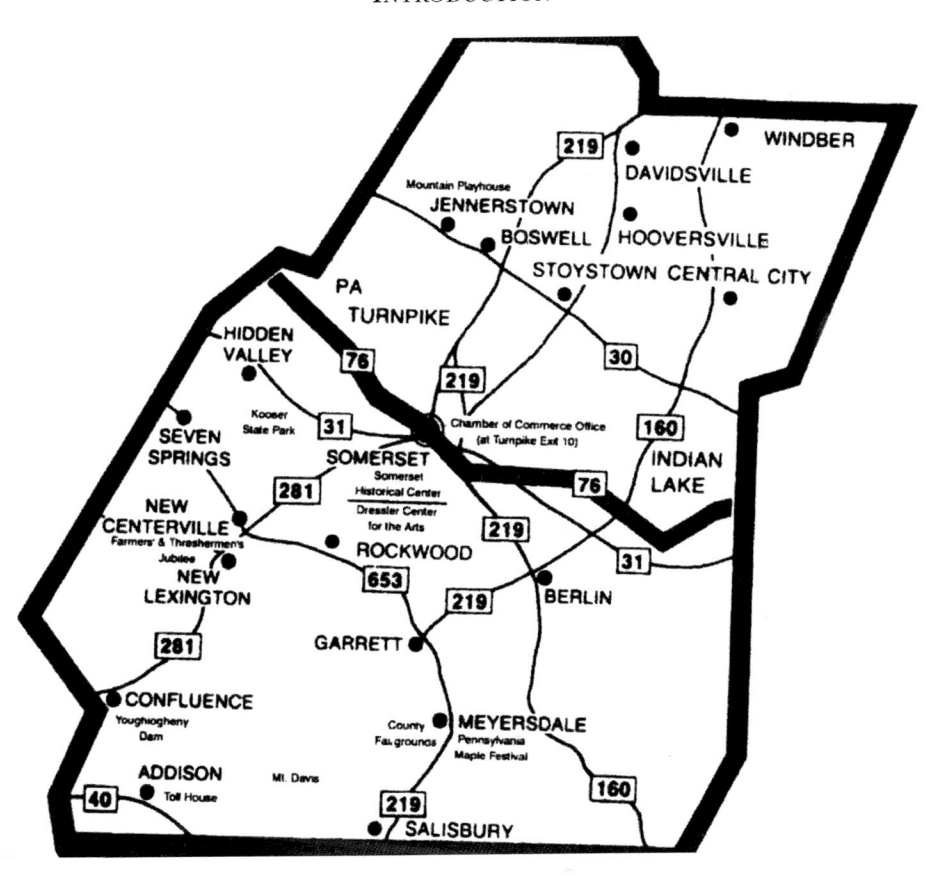

landmark. United Flight 93, traveling at five hundred miles per hour, plunged into a field along Skyline Drive and created a twenty-five-foot-deep crater.

Earlier that morning, in Newark, New Jersey, thirty-three innocent passengers and seven flight crewmembers had boarded the aircraft bound for San Francisco. Forty minutes into the flight four terrorists made themselves known and proceeded to hijack the plane. The aircraft was turned around, headed toward Washington, D.C.

Many passengers used cell phones to inform loved ones of their plight and learned that the World Trade Center in New York and the Pentagon in Washington had been attacked. In what has become a nationally celebrated act of heroism, the passengers onboard fought the terrorists to preserve the plane from striking our national headquarters. Shanksville became a raging inferno when the plane embedded itself twenty-five feet in the ground. Police, firefighters, FBI, Red Cross, Salvation Army and many others rushed to the scene. A leather-bound Bible was found fifteen yards southwest of the crater. It was slightly singed and opened to the first book of Kings, chapters 13 through 15.

The site of the crater, now a cemetery, has become holy ground.

1

Roof Garden of Pennsylvania

Somerset County, in the Laurel Highlands of western Pennsylvania, comprises twenty-five townships, twenty-five boroughs and 1,084 square miles of land. The county was formed from Bedford County on April 17, 1795, as a result of petitions from Harmond Husband and the General Assembly for a new county west of the Alleghenies. On September 12 of that year Somerset, formerly called Brunerstown, was officially declared the seat of justice.

Husband had come to the area in 1771 to escape arrest and death in North Carolina. He said of the Somerset Glades, "Nothing could exceed these plains in beauty!" His home, Coffee Springs House, derived its name from Native Americans living in the area who made a brew from chicory, which grew in abundance on the property. The white man called this "Indian coffee."

In 1794 Husband was among thirteen insurrectionists who were charged with treason and arrested by the commander of the federal militia for their part in the Whisky Rebellion. They were imprisoned for a year in Philadelphia. When released, the seventy-year-old Husband died of fever just as he left Philadelphia.

The Glades are natural meadows surrounding the headwaters of the streams in the center of the county. In 1760 German Baptists settled in the Glades and established a church in the vicinity of Brotherton. The earliest occupations were mining iron ore and coal, farming and lumbering. The town of Somerset grew around the diamond. This was the heart of Somerset in its early days. Surrounded by businesses and hotels, the town featured the Somerset Trust Co., where rental security boxes were initiated. Today this bank is in its fifth generation of presidency within the same family. The diamond market was the first business to accept orders by phone.

The courthouse is a magnificent structure featuring a marble, bronze and walnut interior including a grand staircase, courtrooms and stained-glass windows in the dome. A clock, designed by Howard Clock Company of Lancaster, Pennsylvania, was originally operated by heavy weights. In 1941 it was electrified. The edifice stands 2,190 feet above sea level.

Hotels were popular in and around the Somerset area. People stayed there while their houses were being constructed. Patrons would enjoy each other's company, especially on summer evenings. Somerset House featured a spacious veranda; Belmont House served the traveling public as well as those on business to the courthouse. The Opera House, a frame building on the corner of Englewood and Patriot Streets, was the site of graduations, wedding receptions, recitals and many social functions.

On March 3, 1912, the fire department was officially formed into the Somerset Fire Department. The fire alarm originally was the courthouse bell. The first motorized truck, a LaFrance, was purchased in 1906. The firehouse is beside the Borough Building.

Religion has always played a big part in Somerset County. Initially the German Evangelical/Reformed and the Presbyterian congregations shared a building on land donated by Peter Ankney. Following a mid-century church fire, the German congregation relocated two blocks away and the Presbyterian congregation built across from the courthouse. Molly McKinley, a niece of President William McKinley, was the organist at the new Presbyterian church. During his term, the president came to the Laurel Highlands every summer to spend time with his brother.

In 1895 Somerset County observed its centennial, and the town had certainly grown since its founding. The celebration was executed with much jubilation. Great arches were built above the streets and a fountain placed in the public square—festivities were many. In that same year streetlights were installed and street paving quickly followed. The Pennsylvania Turnpike was built north of the town. This accelerated progress throughout the county but especially in the town itself. It brought in new businesses and diversified cultures.

Somerset was the last of the Pennsylvania counties to have a name from an English shire. It was named for Somersetshire in England.

COFFEE SPRING FARM. ROUTE 31. SOMERSET. PA.

Coffee Springs Farm was originally the home of Harmond Husband, one of Somerset County's earliest inhabitants. Still intact on East Main Street, the house is the oldest in Somerset.

The first courthouse was occupied in 1798 and located on the corner of Center and Patriot Streets. Constructed of stone, it consisted of an office building, the lock-up or jail and the courthouse. It served for a half-century.

The present courthouse was constructed in 1903 on the site of the original building. The thick walls of the basement are native sandstone and the superstructure consists of Indiana limestone quarried locally.

This monument was a tribute to the soldiers who preserved the Union during the Civil War. American Legion Post #210 placed the bronze-cast statue on the corner of North Center and East Union Streets in 1888.

The Volunteer Fire Department was formed in 1865. W.H. Shaddard reorganized the fire department in 1893 and the first firehouse was built on the courthouse grounds. The equipment of that era consisted of hand-operated pumps.

Somerset House on Main Street was a huge three-story hotel with a very large veranda. Located on the Diamond, it was among the first hotels in town.

Belmont Hotel featured floor-to-ceiling windows and a conical round tower. These were indicative of the 1915 era in which it was built. Early drivers observed the rules of parking with the front of the car facing out!

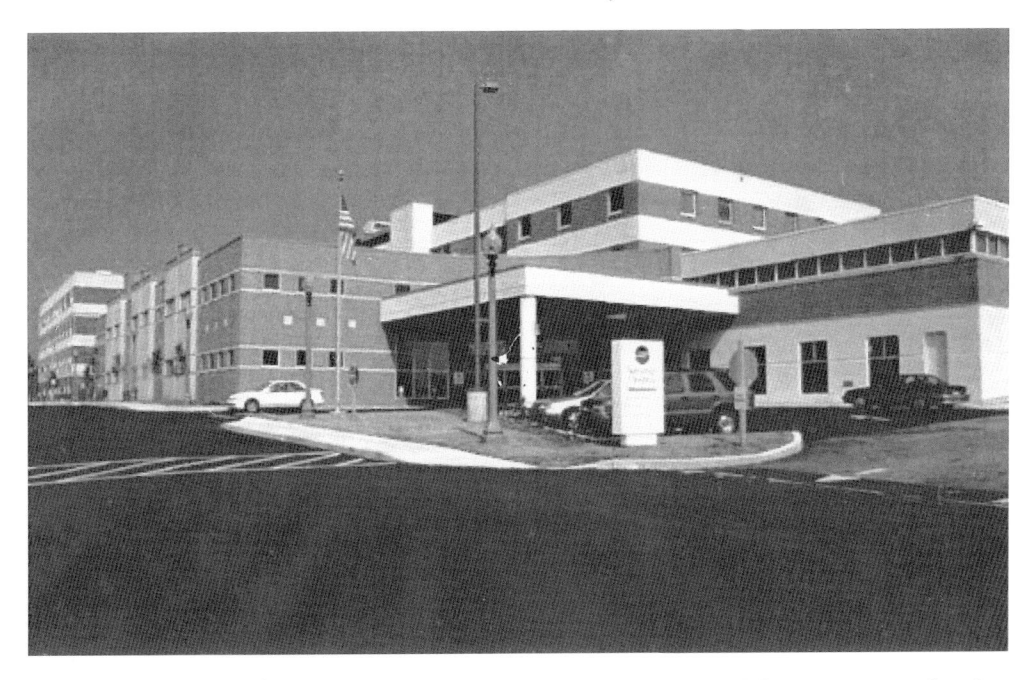

Somerset Hospital became a reality when the private hospital of Dr. Jacob T. Bowman was purchased. Located in the heart of the city it became a 138-bed facility with thirty-five physicians on staff.

Oakhurst Tea Room has been a charming restaurant since 1933 when the Ernest Baker family began serving all-you-can-eat chicken and waffles for fifty cents. Located along Glade's Pike, it has gained a fine reputation for its smorgasbord.

Somerset Trust Company was chartered in 1889 as the First National Bank of Somerset. Today this bank is in its fifth generation of presidency within the same family.

The railroad spurred the lumber and coal industries in the late nineteenth century throughout the Laurel Highlands.

In 1804 a log school was constructed on the southwest corner of Union Cemetery. An academy followed in 1819 and functioned until 1887, when the first three-year high school was established.

West Patriot Street was a residential, landscaped road. The pavers were an early rendition of asphalt paving. This later became a main thruway in Somerset. Paving was often done by owners of stores, homes and businesses.

West Main Street became commercial after the Depression. A hardware store, Bostonian Shoes and a hotel with a Dutch kitchen are on the left. The town clock stands beside Rexall Drugs in this mid-century view.

North Main in 1916 was taking on an aura of commercialism with its many buildings and businesses. The area was once residential and many merchants who built these establishments lived in apartments over them.

Georgian Place dominates the landscape. It was built by Daniel B. Zimmerman, an affluent coal and cattle tycoon. His cattle ranches shipped forty thousand cattle to market annually. He is best known as the county's largest coal operator.

St. Peter's Roman Catholic Church was established in 1920. The parish underwent major mid-century renovations. The church and rectory were constructed on a nine-and-a-half-acre plot. A school and parish houses surround the church.

Above: In 1797 Reverend Henry Geise, a German preacher, came and established the first religious congregation in Somerset. St. Paul's Evangelical Church was established by Peter Ankney, who donated the land.

Left: Waterworks were installed in 1894. Located between North and Union Streets, it was known as Waterworks Pumping Station. Originally it had two wells, but by 1910 it had expanded to ten wells.

The Tam O'Shanters were frequently on demand in Somerset. It was the only organization of its kind in the United States. The Tammies' colorful highland regalia and distinctive presentations gave them an excellent reputation.

Simpson's Auto Service and Garage on Patriot Street was a typical scene of 1920s technology. One gasoline pump served the townsfolk. Note the lead car with its spare tire and isinglass. These served as windows in inclement weather.

Mail Pouch Tobacco advertisements on barns were a very common sight throughout the Laurel Highlands. Barn owners would be paid annually to carry the advertisements that became an icon of early Americana.

2
Jewels in the Mountains

Many towns that had been settled in Somerset County prospered as the county grew and local businesses thrived with the opening of the Lincoln Highway. Stoystown had been founded by Captain Daniel Stoy, a Revolutionary War veteran, who owned all of the land that now makes up the town. Hite House was constructed in 1853, and this busy hotel catered to the travelers of the Lincoln Highway. The intersection Sphect's Corner was one of the major crossroads in the Laurel Highlands.

The cemetery of the International Order of Odd Fellows is preserved in Stoystown. This organization was founded in seventeenth-century England to aid the needy and benefit mankind. At the time, their mission was considered odd, hence the name. Their motto is Friendship, Love, Truth. Odd Fellows came to the United States in 1819 when Thomas Wiley instituted the Washington Lodge in Baltimore. It was the first national fraternity to include women and the first to establish homes for senior citizens and orphans. Its principles are based on the Bible.

Jennerstown was incorporated as a borough in 1874, and named for Dr. Edward Jenners, an English physician who published a process of immunization against the dreaded disease of smallpox. He demonstrated that the disease he called the "speckled monster" was much like cowpox but the scars were smaller. Jennerstown was settled by James Wells, a local farmer who had lost two daughters to smallpox. Wells sent to Dr. Jenners in Glouchestershire, England, for the vaccine, which saved his third daughter's life. He named the town in honor of Dr. Jenners.

Ye Olde Stagecoach Inn was an original stop on the stagecoach line during the pre-motor era. From 1700 into the late 1800s it served many weary travelers. It was a cozy farmhouse built in 1752 and among the earliest bed and breakfast establishments in the nation. Travel was slow, motorcars were in their infancy and the idea of a luxurious drive with dining and sleeping out was a new concept in American life.

In the late 1980s Jennerstown Speedway became part of the NASCAR Winston Cup racing series, now the Nextel Cup Series. The Jennerstown track is one of the fastest half-mile asphalt tracks in the tri-state area.

The Green Gables Restaurant and the natural lake on the Green Gables property add charm to the scenic grandeur of the entire area. Green Gables Restaurant and Playhouse began as a roadside sandwich stand in 1927. It is situated on a seven-acre complex amid exquisite natural beauty. In 1928 it won the national Rockefeller Wayside Stand Contest. The volume of patrons increased and additional rooms were added. The Tuscany Room was designed in 1963 using four giant white oak tree trunks. Each has over three hundred rings indicating their venerable ages. The other rooms are constructed in chestnut and stone taken from the area.

James and Louise Stoughton were the original proprietors, and their family has operated it since 1939. James Stoughton sought ways to attract people to his restaurant during and after the Depression. In 1939 he had a 135-year-old Roxbury gristmill moved beside his restaurant. It was converted to a first-class theater with comfortable atmosphere and climate control. Known as the Mountain Playhouse, it attracts acting professionals from far and wide. It has been a professional summer theater for the past six decades.

White Star Hotel also served as a prominent stop along America's first coast-to-coast road. In later years Larry E. Gindlesperger bought the structure and transformed it into a pleasant senior citizen center.

The origin of the community at Indian Lake goes back to Hurricane Hazel. In 1954 Jim McIntire glanced out from his Rhodes Creek home upon a tremendous lake created by Hazel and an idea was born. The waters receded after three days but a potential dream began to evolve. Between the Laurel and Allegheny Mountain ridges lies an area rich in recreational possibilities. McIntire was no stranger to the area's natural beauty; he made his living at aerial photogrammetry, or taking measurements from the air. He soon formed the McIntyre and Stonycreek Valley Development Corporation.

McIntire began working on a prestigious undertaking. With his corporation, he gathered an assemblage of potential waterfront dwellers who were willing to take a risk and put up their land for stock in the corporation. This land would become part of the development now known as Indian Lake. Another new corporation was formed, known as Allegheny Mountain Lakes Incorporated. The group proposed a limited population resort in a peaceful setting. Today the natural tranquility is retained at Indian Lake and growth continues to take place. The population consists of an intermingling of retirees, working people who make their homes here and those who are permanent lakeside dwellers. It is a friendly and compatible community.

Jewels in the Mountains

In the mid-1700s the virgin mountains, with their scenic vistas, captured the imagination of anyone passing through. When the passersby happened to be artists from Pittsburgh, their imaginations were fired with zeal to translate the atmosphere on canvas. They paused just west of Johnstown and set up their easels. They called the chosen site "Paint" and to this hallowed spot they returned for several years. Their names are lost, as are their paintings, but the chosen, picturesque little hamlet evolved into a borough and later a township, still known as Paint.

On the western fringes of Somerset County rises the highest point in the state of Pennsylvania. It is a boulder 3,213 feet above sea level. Known as Mount Davis, it was first recognized as an area of special significance in 1945 when it became part of a state forest. This mountain was owned by John Davis, and a young engineer friend of his, Harold Bean, discovered it as the highest point in Pennsylvania.

Negro Mountain, also on this site, is located in the center of the Allegheny plateau. Negro Mountain received its name in memory of a black gentleman, the member of a hunting party, who distinguished himself in battle with the Native Americans.

Michael Riddlemoser organized the hamlet of New Baltimore. The area's original Roman Catholic Church, St. John's, was dedicated in 1826. A log rectory was built at the same time. A school was opened in 1830 and the schoolhouse was erected in 1863. Shops and stores sprang up as the town became self-contained. Four Benedictine Sisters taught at the school until 1895 when a law was passed forbidding teachers to wear a dress indicative of religious belief. The history of the parish and town are so intertwined that one includes the other. Riddlemoser's dream was to construct a college—a dream never realized.

In 1870 the Carmelite Fathers were assigned as pastors of St. John's. In 1887 Carmelite students of theology came to continue their studies. A monastery had been erected adjoining the church. It was later converted into a retreat center.

The site of the Quecreek mine rescue is becoming a lasting memorial to all miners. The mining accident occurred at 8:45 p.m., Wednesday, July 24, 2002, when a mining machine hit a wall and broke into an abandoned mine. One hundred and fifty million gallons of water gushed into the Quecreek mine, located on the Arnold farm, six miles north of Somerset. The trapped miners sought refuge in a small, dark chamber and prayed the rescue crew would find them. They took turns tapping with a hammer on a steel bolt—nine taps indicated nine still alive. Relatives and friends of the miners waited in the nearby Sipesville Fire Hall where reports on the progress of the rescue crew came in periodically. The project took tremendous drilling through dense rock. A mesh-like steel cylinder was lowered into the round opening. One by one each miner was evacuated. The last one was brought up at 3:45 a.m. on Sunday, July 28. It was a dramatic rescue that cheered a nation still devastated by the terrorist attacks of September 11, just ten months earlier.

The winds of change have blown through the countryside since Somerset County's founding. Along the Garrett Highway travelers see the ominous-looking structures of the Green Mountain Energy Wind Farm, located on the Decker Farm. The wind farm consists of eight two-hundred-foot-high turbines with constantly rotating blades of ninety-five feet. The windmills can generate electricity with as little as eight-mile-per-hour breezes.

Hite House in Stoystown was a stagecoach stop offering comfortable rooms and a huge ballroom for travelers. Note the band prepared to entertain and the early vintage cars whose riders are assembled in this June 16, 1916 view.

Specht's Corner was the crossroads of Stoystown. The quiet little intersection became a scene of activity on market day. In this view a patriotic celebration is about to begin. Note the many horse-drawn wagons!

Dobson was one of the many merchants who established business early in the century.

Main Street looking south in 1912 with a gasoline station on the right and a white church on the left.

Trostletown Bridge is one of the oldest bridges in Somerset County. Built in 1845 it has a triple span of ninety-two feet. It was restored in 1965 by the Lions Club.

Jennerstown Speedway is an oval, asphalt track. This 1934 Chevrolet coupe was driven for many wins by Pittsburgh driver Joe Viglione. The speedway was originally built with two rustic tracks in the mid-1920s.

Dr. Edward Jenners was an English physician who discovered a smallpox vaccine in 1796. James Wells, a local farmer who had settled in the area, lost two daughters to smallpox. He sent for the vaccine and in gratitude for his last daughter's recovery he named the settlement after Jenners.

The familiar red doors open on the Mountain Playhouse. The theater, operated by the Stoughton family since 1939, offers professional summer performances.

White Star Hotel was owned and operated by the Philson family. It attracted patrons from miles around and soon became a landmark. Tourists along Lincoln Highway enjoyed overnight lodging and dining out. These were new concepts in American life.

Above: Indian Lake is a serene, peaceful site situated in the Laurel Highlands, surrounded by trees, foliage and rustic hillsides. Cottages dot the lakesides and boats cruise the clear rippling waters. An abundance of fish make this their home.

Right: The highest elevation in the state of Pennsylvania, 3,213 feet above sea level, is the top of Mount Davis on Negro Mountain. This observation tower rises 45 feet.

John Davis was a Civil War veteran, school superintendent, surveyor, farmer and minister who owned most of the thirty miles of Negro Mountain. Here he and his son-in-law are checking the Davis holdings.

Seylars Rest House, at Tuscarora Summit, was 2,240 feet above sea level. Note the lookout and the wraparound porches where panoramic views and fresh air were in abundance.

Above: Green Mountain Energy Wind Farm consists of eight huge two-hundred-foot-high turbines with constantly rotating blades of ninety-five feet. These are located along Garrett Road.

Below: Michael Riddlemoser of Baltimore chose a site in the Laurel Highlands for a Catholic settlement. He erected a stone church and plotted the town around it. The area soon became self-contained. The parish later housed a monastery of Carmelite priests.

The covered bridge in New Baltimore adds a rustic charm to the hamlet. It spans a mountain stream and is an attractive site in the area.

The Quecreek mine in Somerset was the scene of a dramatic rescue in July 2002. Communication was established with nine miners trapped 245 feet below the surface of the earth. A square grating covers the rescue hole.

In a moment of triumph all nine miners were brought up to safety. They had been trapped for seventy-seven hours. They were rescued individually in a cylinder such as this.

3
Conemaugh

Conemaugh Township was created in February 1801 in the northwest corner of the county and includes Holsopple, Hooversville, Davidsville, Boswell and Jerome. The word Conemaugh means "long fishing place." Numerous denominations, cultures, backgrounds and countries are represented in the area. The Amish and Mennonite roots remain part of Conemaugh Township.

Holsopple is a small town situated in a bend of the Stonycreek River in northern Somerset County. The town was laid out on the farm of Henry Blough. The railroad station was called Bethel after the nearby Bethel United Brethren Church, built in 1874. The earliest dwelling was built by H.J. Boyt and the first store was opened by Tobias Mishler in 1880. The post office was established in 1881. The little village measured 2,150 feet long and was enclosed by a perimeter of posts.

The first white settlers came to the area around 1780. Among them was Henry Holsopple, who married Susan LeFevre of York, Pennsylvania. They settled in West Virginia and had eight children. Indian raids were common so the white men banded together to provide protection. On one such occasion Henry Holsopple was captured and burned at the stake. His widow took the children back to York, where her father was a merchant.

A soldier, who had been paid for his military service with a land grant, had come into Susan's father's store to buy an overcoat, but he had no money. He paid for the coat with his five hundred acres of land, which Susan's father offered to her. It was necessary to occupy the land in order to retain possession of it, so Susan took the children and immediately went west to claim the land. She built a cabin and made it their permanent settlement. The family became prominent in the area and the Holsopple post office was named after Susan and Henry's son Charles in 1881. Tobias Mishler became the first postmaster and his son, John, was the first baby born in Holsopple.

Lumbering and farming were the chief industries. Later, coal mining became a mainstay. It brought numerous immigrants to town. Many industries sprang up to serve the public as the hamlet became populated. A variety of stores and businesses came into existence. Two doctors served the community for many years. Dr. H.A. Zimmerman became the miners' physician as well as the physician for the Quemahoning Dam construction and for the Baltimore and Ohio Railroad. Holsopple is home to two celebrities: television personality Ron Stevenson, a longtime news director of WJSC; and the first woman elected mayor in Somerset County, Shirley Livingston Jones, elected in 1964.

Hooversville is closely related to Holsopple. In 1794 Casper Ripple obtained a warrant for a tract of land in what is now Hooversville. He was its first settler but the town was not laid out until 1836. The first building lots were sold by Jonas Hoover and the name was adopted in his honor. Hoover was of German-Swiss ancestry. He served two years in the War of 1812 and distinguished himself for bravery under fire. He married the first of three wives and was the first settler to purchase land in what is now Hooversville. He was instrumental in establishing the German Reformed Church.

Hooversville is the location of the Knickerbocker and Oneita coal mines. Their construction transformed the settlement from a small rural hamlet to a thriving borough, incorporated in 1895. In 1876 the post office was established by George Hoover, who became the first postmaster. He was followed by Nathaniel Hamer, who moved the postal service to his store on Main Street. The present post office occupies modern facilities on Barn Street.

By 1848 land was sufficiently cleared for farming and stock raising. The coal industry was launched in 1882 and the Somerset and Cambria branch of the Baltimore and Ohio Railroad was routed through Hooversville. This was the most prosperous era in the town's history. Martha Parka opened the first hotel in 1876 and the second was established by L.B. Brehm. Hooversville became a major coal-producing center with mines including Oneita, Federal, Roger and Knickerbocker.

Trinity Lutheran congregation constructed the first house of worship in the hamlet in 1849. This historic edifice, no longer used for worship, still stands in the Pleasantdale Cemetery. The dedication took place in 1850 with Reverend W.H. Knop as pastor. The parsonage was located first on Water Street then on Church Street. It was here, a half-century later, when the hamlet was growing by leaps and bounds, that the cornerstone of a new Trinity Lutheran Church was laid by Reverend C.H. Watcher. By the 1920s a decision was made to remodel the church and add a multi-storied Sunday school building. The building of modified Gothic art was rededicated in 1924. The main church seats 350 worshippers and the school building holds 200. Reverend Gerald Meyers has been pastor here since 1974.

The first Roman Catholic Mass in St. Anne's Parish, Davidsville/Holsopple, was celebrated in 1911 in a rented hall. It was originally a mission of Holy Family Parish in Hooversville. That same year property was bought from the United Coal

Company and construction on a permanent church began. The church building was completed and dedicated by Bishop Eugene Garvey. In later years a new site was found between Holsopple and Davidsville and a small but impressive edifice of fieldstone and natural wood was constructed on land visible from the highway. In honor of Hooversville's centennial, Johnstown's daily newspaper, the *Tribune-Democrat*, carried the story of the town entitled "The History of a Century." The paper was then sixteen pages in length and sold for two cents per copy.

The swinging bridge of Hooversville became a novelty when it was put into service in 1907. The original footbridge was replaced twice. Patrons were advised to refrain from swinging, running, jumping or loitering on the footbridge and there were penalties for transgressors. The bridges connected two sides of a village divided by Stonycreek River.

Boswell was one of many "company towns" that were developed to provide housing and other community features for coal-mining families. Company stores were an integral part of these communities. Upon entering the store a member of the miner's family presented a slip that was put into a cage and taken to the office. There the clerk—in Boswell it was Aleta Shumaker—crossed off the things she decided the family did not need. Sometimes a second slip was presented that same day by a different member of the family in an effort to get the items that had originally been rejected. The company store offered clothes, shoes, food, appliances and gasoline. This is where a miner's family was to do all their shopping.

Following the close of the mine at Boswell in 1939 the company store, or Quemahoning Supply Company, became the Dorfman and Hoffman Garment Factory. The factory specialized in women's lingerie. Women who worked the factories were the main support for many coal-mining families after the mining jobs were gone. Products from this factory were sold throughout the United States.

During World War II theaters throughout the country featured war reports at the beginning of each show. Boswell was no exception. RKO News supplied the war features. Admission was twenty cents for adults and ten cents for children. When the price was raised to eleven cents it was very difficult to find that extra penny to attend a movie. The last showing at the Boswell theater was in 1956.

Thomas Boswell, founder of the borough of Boswell, had a policy of constructing his houses in a sequential pattern. A timber house was always followed by a brick house then a stone house. If a timber house was consumed in flames the buildings beside it were of brick or stone and would not be damaged. Boswell also named many of his streets after coal company officials. In 1994 the town of Boswell was designated as a National Historic District.

The Ickes Insurance Agency was founded in Boswell in 1906 by Chauncey Semler Ickes at 419 Main Street. In the 1920s it passed on to his son Comfrey Ickes Sr., who operated the business until 1955 when his son, Comfrey Sanford (Squire)

Ickes, took over. Squire and Phyllis Ann McTonic were married on September 21, 1956. They have worked the agency since. At that time the policies were all on twelve clipboards, one for each month. Expansion became an ongoing adventure for them. Now, fourth-generation Christopher Ickes is following in the footsteps of his forefathers with the same integrity, professionalism and dedication the Ickes Agency has always maintained.

Other boroughs in Somerset County also began as company settlements. Jerome became a prosperous neighborhood when the United Coal Company laid it out in 1904. It was located on Jacob Blough's farm. The schoolhouse stands in the center with the old railroad station on the left surrounded by company houses. Windber was a mecca for coal mining! Artifacts pertaining to coal mining are preserved in the Coal Mining Heritage Museum.

Jacob Ease set up the first mills. He was an Amish farmer who settled near Scalp Level. His workers cleared the land and he walked among them instructing, "Scalp the underbrush level with the ground." His words evolved into the name of Scalp Level Road, which has endured.

Hooversville baseball team in 1906 consisted of Murray, Crissey, Williams, Rhoads and J. Hoover. Standing behind them are Seicher, Berkey, King, Johnson, L. Hoover and Lohe. At the very back is J.C. Dull, the manager.

Hooversville was noted for its famous swinging footbridge that spans Stonycreek River. In 1907 it was decided that a footbridge was a necessity in a town divided by a river.

Swinging bridges have always been a source of curiosity to tourists and visitors alike. The footbridge is suspended in such a way that it actually swings while connecting both sides of Hooversville. Note Stonycreek River flowing beneath the bridge.

Hooversville schoolchildren of 1939 enjoyed May Day complete with a maypole. May Day is a harbinger of spring.

A Memorial Day parade makes its way toward the finish line. These parades are dedicated to our servicemen and those who gave their lives defending freedom.

Conemaugh

The first school in Hooversville was built in 1870 on Water Street and a larger edition was constructed on Charles Street a decade later. These were elementary schools.

Trinity Lutheran congregation and Hooversville were born together. Early settlers needed a house of worship and in 1849 a frame building was constructed on land donated by John Weigle.

In 1881 a larger building was constructed at Church and Clark Streets. It was remodeled in 1920 and a multi-storied Sunday school was added. Reverend Gerald L. Myers became the pastor in 1974.

The first Catholic Mass in St. Anne's Parish, Davidsville/Holsopple, was celebrated in 1911 in a rented hall. It was originally a mission of Holy Family Parish, Hooversville. St. Anne's was rebuilt between Holsopple and Davidsville.

Holy Cross Roman Catholic Church was established in Jerome in 1911. The earliest congregation was predominately Polish. Note the rows of miners' homes that form the background.

The United Coal Company at Jerome Mines gave the hamlet prestige. A railroad spur connected the mine to Somerset. It was named for Jerome Coulson, son of the company's founder.

Jerome Hotel was built for visitors and county officials who often came to check on coal mining operations. It later became Bulford's Hotel.

Conemaugh

Above: This barbershop was in the back of the post office in Jerome in 1920, along with a bowling alley and theater.

Right: The company store in Jerome was owned by the Jerome Coal Company. Mining families were expected to obtain all provisions from the company store.

The First National Bank of Jerome was enhanced by window boxes. Initially the vault was buried in the ground when the building was demolished in 1939. Tom Downey is the man on the right; the other three are unidentified. Note the 1920s Studebaker parked beside the bank.

This scene in Jerome following World War I depicts Holy Cross Church on the left with miners' homes. Returning servicemen are standing on the Jerome baseball field. The house at the end of the line belonged to Anthony Mastocola.

This was Main Street, Boswell, in 1904. Somerset House is on the left, followed by Schmucker's hardware store. Miller's barbershop, Keystone Grocery and Merchant's Hotel are on the right. The horse and buggy were still in town.

People's State Bank was the first three-story building in Boswell. Located on Main Street, it was chartered September 10, 1913.

The company store of Boswell was later transformed into a garment factory. Located on Morris Avenue, it also contained at various times Boswell's first post office and a meat market.

The interior of Boswell's company store when it was a garment factory. Garments were shipped to all parts of the country.

The Shaffer Dental Parlor was located on Center Street in 1900. The connotation of the word "parlor" attempted to ease the unpleasantness of the dental work.

Royal Café of Boswell was owned and operated by the Auman brothers. Note the shop next door still has buggies and wagons among its merchandise.

The theater in Boswell featured early and silent motion pictures as well as many plays and entertainments.

Above: A nicolette was part of a bygone entertainment center. Music and speeches could be broadcast outside through a huge megaphone. This was a new innovative and fascinating practice in the early days of the cinema.

Left: Saints Peter and Paul Russian Orthodox Church was constructed in 1915 on Quemahoning Avenue.

Boswell citizens in full regalia celebrate the centenary of the borough in front of Vincent's brick garage, which featured one of the first taxi services in the country.

Ickes Insurance and Financial Services celebrated its centennial as its owners, Phyllis and Squire Ickes, celebrated their golden wedding anniversary.

Above: Windber emerged as a mining town when Charles Berwin established his coal company here in 1874. The Arcadia Theatre was a prominent site of entertainment.

Left: In 1952 Windber schoolchildren presented the coal miners' statue in front of the railroad station. The station has been standing since 1896 when the first passenger train came streaming into town.

4
Land of Sweet Maple

Meyersdale lies in the Casselman River Valley. Its earliest settlers were a tribe of the Monongahela Native Americans, who captured the sweet water from maple trees to make maple sugar. In 1776 John M. Olinger became the area's first white settler and built his home on what is now the corner of Grant Street and Broadway. The Meyers family were very prominent among the early settlers and the town was eventually given their name. (Meyersdale underwent several name changes in its early days.) Peter Meyers was active and influential in his own community and also among the founders of the town of Confluence. He helped bring about the completion of the Pittsburgh and Connellsville Railroad. The post office and railroad station were also placed under the Meyers name.

Early local industries consisted of a blacksmith shop established by John Berger and a tannery on the south side established by Daniel Beachey. Flaugherty Creek divides the north and south sides of Meyersdale. Meyers Mill was established very early in the nineteenth century, a distillery was added in 1803 and a store a few years later. Meyers Tannery was built in 1825. By the 1920s a trolley had been installed along Central Street. It was the pride of the village and a common mode of transportation.

Meyers's home, Maple Manor, is located in Festival Park, and is said to be the oldest house in the area. The manor has become a museum. Each year during Maple Festival time in the spring, it becomes the center of activity when crowds come to visit. The maple industry goes back to Native American times but the first formally organized celebration took place in 1948. The festival includes tours of Maple Manor, maple sugar demonstrations, live stage entertainment, food vendors and historic re-enactments. It spreads throughout the town with a quilt show at the firehouse, agricultural fair exhibits, an old-time medical office and country store. There is also a festival parade and a Maple King and Queen are selected.

Sugar camps sprang up throughout Somerset County when it was discovered that sugar maple trees yield much maple syrup if tapped in early spring. Sap rises from the roots of the tree in very late winter and makes its way up the tree. Holes are drilled in the tree then metal or plastic spiles are driven into the tree. Maple water flows into the keeler bucket or tubing. Sometimes the tree and barrel are connected by tubing that carries the sugar water from the tree to the barrel or bulk tanks. The sugar water or sap is then hauled to the sugar camp to be boiled. It takes seven hundred gallons of sugar water to make fourteen gallons of syrup. One gallon of finished maple syrup will make about seven pounds of taffy or candy.

The sugar camp is a small cabin built for just that purpose. This building is a necessity on all maple-producing farms. The steam produced by the boiling sugar water makes the inside of the camp extremely steamy and damp. The process is watched as the sweet water is boiled and cooked to a syrup then strained and left to settle. This process is repeated several times before candy, taffy or maple sugar emerge. One of the best parts of the process is the spotza, a delicious taffy made by pouring the boiling syrup over ice. It must be done quickly or it disintegrates. Years ago youngsters enjoyed drizzling spotza on snow then eating it.

Meyersdale gained prominence in 1947 when Kate Smith of radio fame sang the praises of Somerset's maple syrup on national airwaves. On one of her shows, Smith remarked how she longed for some really good maple syrup. Several Somerset farmers heard her longings and shipped some to her. Kate announced that it was some of the "sweetest she had ever tasted." Her broadcast was heard around the country and brought crowds of patrons who were interested in the new industry to Meyersdale. People began writing for the syrup. The Meyersdale Chamber of Commerce formed a committee to recognize the industry and handle the demand. The Maple Festival was born.

Eric Arnold has been working with maple products most of his life. His parents, Betty and Robert Arnold, established a maple business near their home in Rockwood. It has become a thriving and prominent enterprise. The Robert Arnold family has been supplying maple products for nearly two decades. Arnold's sugar camp is located along Water Level Road near the town of Rockwood.

When the Baltimore and Ohio rail lines first came through Rockwood in 1871, the area began building up around the railroad. The line continued on to Somerset, and Rockwood emerged as the railroad center of the county. The tranquil sound of birds and the rustle of wind in the trees were broken by the shrill whistles as the locomotives made their way into remote settlements and thriving villages on the mountains.

Hotels were prominent in the area. Rockwood House was constructed in 1882 by D.H. Wolfersberger. Situated opposite the Baltimore and Ohio Railroad station, it was considered the travelers' hotel. The Rockwood was famous for its insistence on temperance. Buckman House had several proprietors—such names as M. Marette, F. Robinson, S. Paze and C.J. McSpadden are imbedded in its history. In 1930 E. Miller took it over and Mrs. Blanche Ringe opened a rooming house in the building. In 1946 Norman Bedford, president of Olbo stores, and Floyd Pritts, a barber, remodeled the building into apartments.

In 1928 Miller's Restaurant was a prestigious site where natives gathered and travelers dined. The restaurant was established in 1870 by Joseph Miller, a Civil War veteran who had been wounded at Newmarket, Virginia, in 1864. His father, Daniel Miller, had been a wagon maker who had come from eastern Pennsylvania. As a civilian, Miller taught school and was a clerk for the House of Representatives in Harrisburg.

Miller's Department Store, one of the oldest businesses in town, stood on the southeast corner of Main and Market Streets. Originally built as a hotel in 1916, it later became a store with a huge bowling alley in the basement.

In 1946 President Harry S. Truman delivered a speech at the Rockwood railroad station. He was on a campaign tour. It was a red-letter day in Rockwood when he arrived.

Maple Manor was the home of Peter Meyers (1807–1870), for whom Meyersdale was named. The home is a prominent feature in the Pennsylvania Maple Festival, held every spring since Kate Smith, the famous singer, sang the praises of Meyersdale's maple syrup.

The sportsir where maple sap is boiled on the Arnold farm. Maple farms require these structures because of the intense steam needed in the process of making maple products. The temperature and steam would damage the interior of homes.

This is a bygone method of maple syrup production. Mr. Robert Arnold is gathering wood to keep the steam boiling. Wood was once the sole source of heat in the camps.

Above: Eric and Betty Arnold, with visitors, keep vigil over the boiling syrup. It is put through several boiling processes before it is cooled.

Right: Teresa Migot is displaying the maple taffy, which is about to be placed in a cool atmosphere to set.

Betty Arnold looks on while a visitor stirs the thickened syrup into maple sugar. Notice the consistency.

Land of Sweet Maple

Melissa, Theresa Migot, Betty Arnold, Brittany and Miss Aurant sample the spotza. Betty is holding a cup of ice water, which is necessary to cool the spotza.

Jugs are prepared to ship the maple syrup to market.

Eric Arnold, Maple Sugar Champion of Somerset County, won the 2002 Maple King title in the annual Maple Festival. Arnold also won the Maple Syrup Championship in 1997, 1998 and 2000.

Land of Sweet Maple

Meyersdale's Grant Street in the 1920s when the trolley was the common mode of transportation. The postcard is dated November 16, 1914.

North Street in Meyersdale was a rustic, tree-lined road. This postcard was sent from Gleco on August 15, 1908, and bears a one-cent stamp.

Rockwood Hotel was constructed in 1882 by D.H. Wolfersberger. Situated directly across from the B&O Railroad station, it was considered the travelers' hotel. The Rockwood was famous for its insistence on temperance.

Buckman House was built by Samuel Buckman on the corner of Main and Market Streets in 1894. He was a contractor and bridge builder who came to Rockwood in 1880. He had previously built the Merchants Hotel.

Artifacts featured in the Mill Shoppe include a wicker pram of early nineteenth-century vintage, a victrola (a windup musical phonograph) and a potbelly stove like those that warmed many a home and business.

John Miller, proprietor of Miller's Clothing Store, is on the right and James McPar is in the center beside an unidentified customer. Suspenders are displayed in the window. These were very popular early in the twentieth century.

The inside of Miller's store was always cozy and warm. It was a gathering place where news of the day was swapped. The neatly arranged shelves held everything anyone could want.

Walkers Family Shop with straw hats in the window. The lads on the left are unidentified; Joseph Miller, George Ott and Jacob Schultz are on the steps. Danny and Ray Miller are on the right side.

Miller's Department Store stood on the southeast corner of Main and Market Streets. C.A. Miller is one of the oldest merchants in Rockwood.

Main Street in 1882 featured a watering trough for horses, seen at the left of the photograph. This was provided in most villages.

The round house at Rockwood was constructed in 1910 to service locomotives and railroad cars. Rockwood became a railroad town as the area grew around the railroad.

A train returns to Rockwood. A water tank and the railroad station form part of the complex. The control tower, known as WT, was built in 1905. This was a communications block station, a dispatch center that directed railroad traffic.

Snyder's bakery on Market Street in Rockwood, with its many employees and fleet of delivery trucks.

The Rockwood Band of 1910 is entertaining on the corner of Main and Market Streets. This was a common practice in many small towns.

Rockwood has had its share of parades. A Memorial Day parade honoring our war heroes is an annual event.

Backyard gatherings were common. Friends gathered to chat, read, recreate and play games. This group consists of Mary Jane Wolf, Ida Bittner, Lucile McSpadden, Sarah Cordie, Olive, J.C. Farling, Blanche Bittner and two unknown. Second row: Pearl McCormick, Mrs J.C. McSpadden, Mae Bittner, Pearl Saunders, Sadie McSpadden, Mrs. Aaron Bittner and Charles Bittner.

Land of Sweet Maple

A Sunday afternoon drive in the country was a novelty to adults and children alike. At the turn of the century the horse and buggy gave way to the horseless carriage.

Casselman River flows through a mountain valley between Rockwood and Meyersdale. Originally a narrow railroad spanned the river. It connected to a bank rising nearly two hundred feet above the river. Today many bridges span the Casselman River.

5
Curiosities and Resorts

Among the wonders of Somerset County is the little town of Turkeyfoot. It was established in 1848 and named by Native Americans. A part of this area takes the shape of a turkey foot as a result of the meeting or confluence of three bodies of water: the Youghiogheny River, the Casselman River and Laurel Creek, which also form the borough of Confluence. Nestled in the Appalachian Mountains, the little town of Confluence is not only a land of year-round recreation but it is also perhaps the best-kept secret of these mountains. Located on the western border of the county it is well known for white-water kayaking, fishing and boating.

Salisbury was founded by Joseph Markley in 1795. Early Dutch settlers named the settlement Salsburrich because salt deposits were found in the area. It became Salisbury with the coming of the post office. The Salisbury viaduct was an engineering success when it spanned the Casselman River Valley in 1912. It was the longest railroad bridge in the country at 1,908 feet. At some places the viaduct is 100 feet above the valley floor. Beginning at the eastern end of the valley, an electric crane placed the girders that were then welded into place. On January 18, 1912, the first train crossed the viaduct. Spectators lined both sides of the bridge. A flatcar and steam engine made the initial trip to the cheering applause of the crowds. The viaduct served for over six decades, but the bridge was destined to be recycled into a recreational project. In 1975 it was renovated; its crossties were removed, a concrete deck and railings installed and it became part of the Allegheny Highlands Trail.

St. Petersburg Toll House in Addison was built in 1818 along the National Road. Known as the "Historic Road that Built the Nation," the road became a link among eastern coastal states because it led to the development of lands west of the Alleghenies. It became prominent due to economic and political concerns and western migration.

Ninety miles of the National Road cut through the southwestern corner of Pennsylvania. It was the first multi-state federally funded road and was heavily traveled with Conestoga wagons, farmers, politicians and stagecoaches. Taverns sprang up and towns developed. Then the horseless carriage made its noisy appearance. The ridges of the Alleghenies saw the rise of many roadhouses. Autos had to climb steep grades and were often overheated. Roadhouses offered travelers a place to dine, sleep and obtain gas while waiting for their car to cool.

Carl Graham Fisher was an entrepreneur with keen imagination. He conceived the idea of a transcontinental highway across the United States. He had perfected the installation of headlights on cars, transformed a Florida swamp into a first-class resort in Miami and now dreamed of linking the Atlantic coast to the Pacific. He elicited financial help from Frank Seiberling, president of Goodyear, and Henry Joy, president of Packard Motor Industry. In 1913 the Lincoln Highway Association was formed with Joy as president. He suggested the name and Fisher liked the patriotic ring.

The road began in Times Square, New York City, and terminated 3,389 miles later in San Francisco. The most direct route was chosen, to the dismay of governors who wanted the road to run through their states. Many preexisting roads were linked together to make up the Lincoln Highway, including part of Somerset's Forbes Road.

The project was dedicated on October 31, 1913. In 1926 the country instituted a system of numbered highways. The famous roadway retains its name and is also known as Route 30. Unique attractions along the route include a round barn, a huge coffee pot and a ship.

In 1930 Herbert Paulson established a small business at Look Out Point in Schellensburg, where Bedford and Somerset Counties meet. He created a sensation when he fashioned a castle hotel situated 2,464 feet above sea level. The next year he built a ship around it, giving his hotel the appearance of an ocean steamer. The deep chasm below gave the illusion of an oceanic setting. Seemingly situated on the water, the ship hotel was suspended from a mountain ridge. A service station was part of the ship complex—it sat below the towering sedimentary rock and was known as Freedom Gas and Oil. Paulson's king of curiosities rode the crest of the Alleghenies on a wild hilltop and was a Lincoln Highway attraction for seven decades.

But when a "magic" road was considered that would bypass towns, villages, traffic lights and all those little obstructions that delay traffic, the Lincoln Highway lost its status as the thruway of Pennsylvania. In 1883, William K. Vanderbilt had envisioned a high-speed rail across Pennsylvania connecting the east with Pittsburgh and points west. It was conceived as the South Penn Railroad. The rail bed was laid, but Vanderbilt could not obtain competitive freight rates from the railroad so he began to construct the railroad on his own. Two years later, political and financial obstacles forced Vanderbilt to discard his railroad dream and in 1885 he left four and a half miles of tunnels and many miles of graded roadbed abandoned.

In 1930 citizens lobbied the Pennsylvania legislature to consider an all-weather highway using Vanderbilt's abandoned project. This led to the formation of the Pennsylvania Turnpike Commission. Today the turnpike is 531 miles in length with fifty-nine fare collection facilities, twenty-one Sunoco convenience plazas, two travelers' information centers, twenty-one maintenance facilities, eight state police barracks and five tunnels.

In 1932, Adolph Dupre, a forester by trade and innovator by nature, brought his bride, Helen, to a mountain retreat. He built a little cabin on land similar to their native Bavaria. Adolph had been groundskeeper and farmhand for the Mellon family on their Ligonier estate. He knew how city folk appreciated relaxation. Adolph and Helen could not move all the snow that fell on their two acres so they decided to take advantage of it, opening their property as a ski lodge. A resort began to take shape when the stream of skiers grew in leaps and bounds. However, the long trudge uphill was a deterrent to some skiers. Adolph invented and installed the first mechanical rope tow in Pennsylvania. Using a Packard truck engine he secured with boards, he put its power to work on the slopes. By 1935, with wooden plank skis and leather bindings, guests skied the slopes of Seven Springs and pioneered the sport in these mountains.

To accommodate the crowds Adolph built the Tydol House, a combination club and dining hall complete with guest rooms. It became a center of social activity. He then built twenty cabins of native stone and wood over the next two decades. He designed these cabins himself in unique beauty and style. The original ski lodge was located on the site of the present lodge at the base of Wagner Slope. Seven Springs Farm evolved from a private club to a resort opened to the public in 1937. In that year the main lodge was completed, affording greater accommodation to enthusiastic crowds. Throughout the 1940s Adolph continued to build cabins while Helen tended to their Brown Swiss cattle.

The mountain elevation is 2,990 feet with a base of 2,240 feet. The average natural annual snowfall is 105 inches. But when Mother Nature doesn't provide, snow is created and blown on the slopes. Long ago, Seven Springs was equipped to survive snow droughts with the installation of more than 900 snow towers supplemented by snow cannons. The numerous pipe-like objects that dot the slopes are actually snow makers. The system pumps thirty thousand gallons of water per minute through 956 towers. This covers 95 percent of the 275 skiable acres. Water from Lake Tahoe, combined with air, creates the snow. In favorable weather the system produces 1 foot of snow on 54 acres in five hours.

There is one high-speed six-passenger lift, three quads, five triple, four tubing tows, a conveyor and two magic carpet conveyor lifts. When chairlifts return from the mountaintop they revolve on cables in preparation for the return ascent. The chairlift capacity at Seven Springs is 22,200 skiers per hour. Herman Dupre,

Adolph's son, invented the first chairlift and introduced snowmaking equipment in 1960. He invented and patented the Millennium Snowmaking Gun that is used nationwide. He owns Snow Economics, Inc., a world-renowned snowmaking company. Seven Springs is the official testing ground for new products.

The two-acre plot of land on which the original cabin was constructed in 1932 expanded to a sprawling 5,500 acres accommodating 5,000 guests in the year-round resort. It annually attracts a half million skiers and tens of thousands of all-season guests. A high-rise hotel dominates the beautiful, rustic landscape. Completed in 1972 it accommodates 313 guests. Seven Springs Convention Center offers a year-round sylvan retreat.

Rustic stone bridges such as this one, that crosses Clear Run Creek, gave way to a more modern trend that could carry the horseless carriage over the streams and creeks of Somerset County. This postcard of 1915 bears a one-cent stamp.

St. Petersburg toll house in Addison, Pennsylvania, is an octagonal building built in 1818 along the National Road. Constructed of native stone, it was the home of William Condon, toll keeper, who resided there with his family.

Forbes Inn was established on the Lincoln Highway in Stoystown to serve a traveling public who were not accustomed to such luxury. Automobiles were in their infancy. The inn was named for Brigadier General John Forbes, the British general who captured Fort Duqusene.

Left: Lincoln Highway signs became an icon on the American scene. They were among the first road signs in the country and bring a touch of nostalgia to those who remember the golden age of the Lincoln Highway.

Below: This scenic ribbon of highway wound its way over mountains and through valleys and centuries of history. When completed in 1925 the famous Lincoln Highway stretched 3,389 miles from coast to coast.

Curiosities and Resorts

Above: The picturesque road winds its way along the tableland of the mountain and seems to ascend into the horizon. It was the nation's first transcontinental highway. The unpaved roads were not yet a deterrent in fine weather.

Below: The Lincoln Highway assumes many different names as it passes through small towns. The most popular is Main Street. It crosses through five Pennsylvania counties. Note the luxurious convertible of the 1920s.

The Grand View Hotel was established by Herbert Paulson in 1930 in the semblance of a castle. Look Out Point is 2,464 feet above sea level in the heart of the Alleghenies.

Paulson fashioned his castle into the likeness of a floating ship. The "SS Grand View Hotel" was a successful tourist venue when it opened May 29, 1932, at Look Out Point. The chasm below gave the impression of a ship sailing.

Curiosities and Resorts

Grand View Hotel was the only steamboat in the mountains! It was a major attraction when complete. Its telescope, which was a new innovation, gave tourists an opportunity to view three states and seven counties.

The huge deck on front of the "steamer" afforded a panoramic view of the mountains. The scenery in this area is exceptionally magnificent.

Left: Freedom Gas and Oil was established across from the Ship of the Alleghenies to service its patrons. Nestled below towering sedimentary rock, it retains a lookout of the castle.

Below: The Pennsylvania Turnpike was dubbed "Dream Highway" when it opened in 1940. The time had come for faster travel on paved roads. The "magic" road bypassed villages, traffic lights and all those little obstructions that delay traffic. It cut driving time in half.

Curiosities and Resorts

Right: This scene demonstrates the depth of the mountain cut. The sign on the left indicates St. John's Church, New Baltimore. The turnpike encountered a plateau through Somerset County.

Below: The building of the Salisbury Viaduct was a project of engineering expertise. It was constructed with huge iron girders stretching nineteen hundred feet across the Casselman River Valley, the mainline of the Baltimore and Ohio Railroad and Route 219.

Seven Springs Resort is nestled in the picturesque Laurel Highlands. It is the largest resort in the state and was established when Adolph and Helen Dupre purchased a two-acre site at Champion, Pennsylvania, in 1930. The atmosphere was akin to their homeland, Bavaria.

Adolph takes his family and their friends around Seven Springs Farm in the very early days of its establishment.

Curiosities and Resorts

Helen's Restaurant is the original home of the founding family. Built by Dupre in 1930 as a Bavarian cabin, it was converted by Helen into a fine restaurant where she served delicious meals.

This rustic sink was installed by Dupre when the cabin was built. He used stone from the highlands to create the sink and then equipped it with running water. Today plants are kept in the sink.

Above: A single skier takes to the slopes. The original lodge and warming hut are in the background. Seven Springs grew in leaps and bounds. By 1948 the 2 acres were advanced into 5,500 acres.

Left: Two skiers, Tyler Davis and Herman Dupre, ski the huge Wagner Slope. At age eighty-four, Davis still serves on ski patrol. Ski patrol attendants handle mishaps or accidents on the slopes. There are three such sites open during ski season.

Opposite below: Long ago Seven Springs was equipped with a system of snow towers and cannons to survive erratic snowfall whims. Herman Dupre invented the snowmaking equipment. In favorable weather the system produces one foot of snow on fifty-four acres in five hours.

Curiosities and Resorts

Above: Snowy slopes abound! On a typical winter morning crowds gather for a day of recreation. Patrons come from all over the East Coast for fun at the resort.

Above: Paul Close is a ski lift operator who sets the chairlift into action. Skiers board on ground level and ski off at mountain level. The chairs seen here are going up the mountain. When they return they revolve on cables in preparation for their next ascent.

Left: In autumn when leaves are in majestic array chairlifts operate just for the ride of it. The chairlift carries spectators to the mountaintop, affording them an opportunity to view some of the most majestic foliage in the Laurel Highlands.

Curiosities and Resorts

Hidden Valley Four Seasons Mountain Resort is known by its clock tower. The resort dates back to 1950, when George and Helen Parke converted their many acres of rolling mountain wilderness into a multi-seasonal resort.

SOMERSET COUNTY, PENNSYLVANIA

HIDDEN ✸ VALLEY

Moonbeams illuminate the shining, snow-covered mountain on this promotional postcard for Hidden Valley Resort. This resort covers acres of charming mountainside including a golf course and a conference center.

6
Berlin in America

In the 1780s, the Calvinist/Reformed and Lutheran congregations in Pennsylvania were desirous of settling new territory. They came upon a spring, camped there and soon formed a permanent settlement that later became the borough of Berlin, the oldest town in Somerset County. This spring is the source of the Stonycreek River, which flows into the Conemaugh, Allegheny, Ohio and Mississippi Rivers and on to the Gulf of Mexico.

An early record indicates Jacob Keefer was granted forty acres in trust for the Calvinist and Lutheran congregations at the headwaters of the Stonycreek River. The settlement was laid out in 1784 by Jacob Kimmel and surveyed by Alexander H. Philson. The borough was incorporated in 1827. In later years the borough lines were changed to the present-day boundaries.

In 1760 George Martin brought German Baptists from Antrim Township and settled a small area known as Brotherton. In the assemblage were three brothers: George, Harry and James Brotherton. The settlement was named for the trio. Large migrations of Germans desirous of freedom from the impending war between the colonists began populating the area. The settlers consisted chiefly of Quakers and Mennonites who did not believe in taking up arms. Recently freed from the bonds of government, taxation and war, they sought freedom in the American wilderness. They were a religious people, and each denomination built its own house of worship.

When the new Church of the Brethren was completed in Berlin, the borough used the original white church building for their meetings. The first pastor was Michael Stretch, ordained in the Church of St. Michael, Philadelphia. The congregation split in 1812 because settlers who lived near the Casselman River wanted a church closer to their homes. They established Mt. Zion Reformed Church.

In 1719 German Brethren migrated to Germantown, Pennsylvania, and others followed. Peck Becker organized the local congregation in 1723 as the German Baptist Church. This dwelling became inadequate for the increasing congregation and a larger building was needed for the love feast celebrations. A building was erected to accommodate both services.

In 1785 the first stores in the hamlet of Berlin were opened. The earliest were those of John Fletcher, Robert Philson and Adam Miller. Goods were hauled over the mountain from the east by packhorse and later by wagon. Pioneers were forced to depend on their own resources. There were no passable roads, a few foot trails left by Native Americans and a mountain barrier between the little settlement and cities to the east. It took ingenuity and perseverance to obtain the bare necessities of life such as food, clothing and implements.

Dr. John Kimmel had been a colonel in the Pennsylvania militia. He owned a store and the Black Horse Tavern. He had a cow but no barn so the cow had to be milked in the kitchen during winter. The inn was bought by William and Sarah Hillegass, who operated a tavern between 1883 and 1918. They kept overnight guests and stagecoach travelers who were traveling the Glades Pike.

In 1795 Fred Groff bought the building on Main Street on the Lower Diamond that housed the Schmidtbarndt blacksmith shop and established a store. General stores sold nearly everything one might need—it was one-stop shopping. Groff placed a penny scale beside the door. The building later became a Wheelwright store where chairs were made, then a barracks before finally becoming a residence. The barracks were used as a warehouse until it was sold to the bank.

Groff wasn't the only merchant in Berlin. Heffley Hardware Store stood beside Mike Dively's little restaurant and ice cream shop and Clarence Beech, Jacob Stutzman (owner) and Donald Maust ran the Stutzman store.

Snyder's Potato Chip Company had its beginning when Edward Snyder visited Saratoga, New York, in 1853. While dining in the Grand Union Hotel he observed a request to slice the potatoes so thin and fry them so they would be crisp. Thus the potato chip was born. Snyder brought the idea back to his Hanover home and found the project successful. He relocated to Berlin because the best potatoes for chipping grew in Cambria and Somerset Counties.

The Berlin Brothers Valley Industrial Association was formed as Snyder's company expanded. The chips were originally hand packed into kraft paper bags that had the product name printed on them. In 1940 aluminum bags were put into use. A mechanical potato peeler was acquired and this sent production soaring. The new snack was an immediate and sensational success. Today Snyder's is a division of Birds Eye Foods and still a thriving producer of the most delicious chips.

In the late 1800s Plank Road construction got underway with an early attempt at paving a road. In the days before pavers, asphalt or cement, wooden planks were arranged crosswise and pinned down by wooden spikes. The unusual road became a source of adventure, legends and escapades. It enjoyed heavy traffic, stagecoaches and lumbering freight wagons. A little schoolhouse was constructed along this route. Claude Baumaster was the instructor.

The National House was a very prominent hotel on Berlin's Main Street. The spacious facility advertised day boarders, weekly boarders, good accommodations, reasonable rates, fine stables and an abundant supply of feed for the animals. During the festivities of Old Home Week all hotels were filled and natives offered to take in boarders from out of town. People gathered on Main Street to watch the upcoming parade. Many businesses designed decorative floats by way of advertisement. Groff Brothers had a wagon pulled by horses and painted on the side was the slogan "The Long Store with Short Prices."

In military camps across the country, and abroad, a spirit of jubilation reigned on November 11, 1918, with the signing of the armistice. In Berlin the return of servicemen was heralded with welcoming festivities and celebrations. Stars were sewn on the buntings, one for each soldier, sailor or marine who served in the military. The Fife and Drum Corps marched in the parade. The corps has long been part of Berlin—the original Fife and Drum Corps was organized in 1782 under the direction of Mr. George Johnson.

A very early record indicates that in 1786 Jacob Keefer was granted land in trust for the Calvinistic and Lutheran congregations in the area that became Berlin.

Above: Pius Spring was discovered when pioneers were sent westward over the Alleghenies to establish a new settlement. A little springhouse was built over the spring.

Below: The *Berlin Record*, Berlin's first newspaper, was initially housed on Main Street's Upper Diamond. F.G. Chorpening was editor. The first issue was published on November 25, 1885.

Above: The Black Horse Tavern was occupied by Dr. John Kimmel, who established his medical practice in 1791 in an area known as Dividing Ridge.

Below: Samuel Philson and Charles A.M. Krissinger established the banking business of Samuel Philson & Co. on Main Street. *Left to right*: Anne Philson, Jim McCabe, H. Bunn Philson and Robert Philson.

Above: Levi Shoemaker was the first inhabitant of Berlin to reach the centenary mark. He celebrated his hundredth birthday on January 12, 1912. This photo was taken with his friends when he was ninety-seven. *Seated, left to right*: Dr. H. Gary, Charles Ream, Levi Shoemaker, Emil Masters and J.S. Heffley. *Standing*: Dr. W.A. Garman, W.A. Powell, Alex Musser, Jay Ross and William Ream. Shoemaker was a former sexton in both the Lutheran and Reformed churches.

Left: The original St. Michael Lutheran Church at Pine Hill dates back to 1789. Initially the congregation worshipped in the schoolhouse. Nicholas Coleman donated one acre of land where the new church building was built.

The Old Brotherton Valley German Baptist Church was located on Brotherton Road.

St. Luke's Mountain Reformed Church with its stained-glass windows has a large congregation. The colonial-type building was constructed in 1861 and dedicated in October of that year.

Plank School took its name from Plank Road, which was a curiosity of the nineteenth century.

Merchants, clerks and customers in front of Groff's general store. *Left to right*: Ted Miller, Fred Groff, Clyde Dickey, Edward Stuck, Ena Groff, Gertrude Deeter Moore and Pearl Pritz. Note the penny scale.

Interior of Fred Groff's store. The men, from left to right, are W. Harvey Divel, C. Weller Saylor, George Collins and Fred Groff. The women pictured are Susan Deeter Garman, Mollie Muhlenberg, Laura Engle, Minnie and Cober Manges.

Pictured here in front of Groff Department Store are (left to right) Ted Miller, office clerk; Fred Groff, owner; Clyde Dickey, shoe department manager; Ed Stuck, in charge of the grocery department; and Gertrude Deeter, Ena Groff and Pearl Pritz.

Jacob Stutzman's general store, prominent in the 1920s, was one-stop shopping In this photo the clerks gather around the radiator to keep warm This was the only source of heat in the building.

Heffley Hardware, which dates back to 1899, featured a hitching post where horses waited for their owners. Mike Dively's restaurant and ice cream shop, next door, was a popular spot.

Berlin in America

Inside Heffley Hardware Store in early 1900s. Robert Heffley, owner, is on the right and clerk Joseph Evil is behind the counter serving customers.

Edward Levy awaits customers in his store on Main Street. The huge phonograph player and the hanging electric lights were new innovations early in the century. A display of postcards stands on the counter.

The White Star double barn was erected by H.J. Glessner in 1899. It was later split in half in a snowstorm when snow collected in the center of the roof. Nevin Croner is on horseback.

Old Home Week was celebrated on the Diamond in 1908. Bent saplings formed the arches and ropes suspended from the central pole were wrapped with spruce twigs. The National House stands on the left.

Main Street was gaily decorated during Old Home Week. Flags and buntings deck the parade route. The climax of festivities was an ox roast held on the Lower Diamond.

Old Home Week in 1937 featured parades and floats. Berlin natives returned for the celebration and everyone had a good time. Hotels were filled and folks living in town took visitors in.

Somerset County, Pennsylvania

The 110th Regiment Company C joined in the 1919 Memorial Day parade. The regiment was organized in November 1873 as the tenth regiment of the infantry whose mission was to capture the enemy or assist in doing so.

The motor trolley assured passengers fresh air and transportation.

Opposite below: The 1959 Berlin Fife and Drum Corps. *Front row, left to right*: John Bennett, James Stuck, Vernon Lyons, Ralph G. Landis, Wayne Coughenour and Richard Platt. *Second row*: Frank W. Pritts, Richard Poorbaugh, J. Wesley Ross, James Coughenour, Lewis Polly Fisher and George Walters. Third row: Jack Harding, George Fisher, Ross Hendershot, James Robert Flick and Floyd Miller.

Opposite above: The Fife and Drum Corps performed in the 1950 parade. Seen here are Lewis Fisher, Ralph Landis, Charles Cook and Richard Johnson.

Flax is manufactured for its fiber. It is spun into linen for clothing, rope, thread and paper. Flax seeds contain linseed oil and are used widely in the production of paint and varnishes. Clyde Walker stands on the right of this parade float.

Coca-Cola became popular in the late nineteenth century.

The little hamlet of Brotherton was one of the earliest settlements in what is now Somerset County. The Bauermaster farm contained the post office and Brotherton Brethren Church.

7

Shanksville

Shanksville is a quiet little hamlet in Somerset County with a magnetism that kept many natives in the area. Situated eleven miles east of Somerset, one of its earliest settlers was Christian Shank. He bought the entire tract of what is now Shanksville for twenty dollars in 1798. He then established a water-powered sawmill and gristmill on the banks of the Stonycreek River. The post office was opened in 1878 with Josiah Brant as first postmaster. There was no rural delivery; 244 mailboxes were installed and every citizen of the hamlet was expected to have one.

Although somewhat diversified the little settlement remains much the same as it has been for centuries. Half the population is retired and many townsfolk were born in or near the hamlet. The little town once comprised a country doctor, blacksmith shop, drugstore and a wagon shop opened by John R. Marher. There were two hotels, one of which still stands today. One small general store graces the hamlet. Once owned by Ida Spangler, it is now under the proprietorship of the King family. The old fire hall, which has become a social center, stands on a prominent corner. Steeples of the churches pierce the skyline.

Then came a moment that would forever change not only Shanksville but also the entire United States. Houses trembled, cupboards rattled, a deafening explosion shook the earth. A tremendous plume of smoke billowed into the heavens and obstructed the bright fall sunshine as it rose from a field on Skyline Drive. The impact of a Boeing 757 that buried itself twenty-five feet in the ground was felt and heard for miles around. United Airlines Flight 93 had left Newark International Airport at 8:42 a.m., bound for San Francisco. Forty minutes later the cockpit was hijacked by terrorists who intended to redirect the plane to attack Washington, D.C. Passengers onboard used their cell phones to call loved ones and learned the news that the twin towers in New York had been attacked. The passengers were herded to the back of the plane and told there was a bomb onboard. As the aircraft turned east over Cleveland heading for Washington, a struggle ensued and the aircraft went down in a Shanksville field at 10:03 a.m. It was a disaster of such magnitude that it forever transformed the quiet, rural Stonycreek Township into a national cemetery.

The disaster brought many people together, united as one regardless of race, color or creed. Religion came to the forefront. Memorial services were conducted by nearly every denomination throughout the land. The United Methodist, Lutheran and Assembly of God congregations in Shanksville banded together. During the first few weeks following the disaster the crash site was off limits.

Shanksville devised its own memorials. The first were visible along the rural roads leading to the site and at the end of Main Street in Shanksville. These mementoes were moved to the Flight 93 temporary memorial when it opened in early spring of 2002. It was located on the hilltop a few hundred yards from where the disaster occurred. Large boards were installed where visitors could place artifacts or write messages.

An ambassador program of local men and women who staffed the site was initiated. They assisted visitors, showed pictures and gave directions. By summer 2002 there were forty-one volunteers in the ambassador program. Within the first year the temporary memorial had been visited by tens of thousands from all walks of life and from all over the world. A flag was placed in the field marking the actual site where the plane went down. The ambassadors were on duty and a police guard kept vigil at all times. A parade on July 4, 2002, was devoted to honoring the victims of September 11.

A golden steel angel was sculptured by Lei Hennessey, an artist from the state of Washington. She sculpted similar angels for Ground Zero and the Pentagon. Our angel weighs twelve hundred pounds and is twenty feet tall. The truck driver who transported these angels across the United States was Dave Owen. The angels brought Lei and Dave together. They were married beneath the angel on September 11, 2002.

Coming over a hill on Skyline Drive one catches a first glimpse of the temporary memorial. It is adorned with heartfelt tributes and mementoes left by family members and visitors to the site honoring the heroes of Flight 93. Stars were placed on the plywood board, one for each passenger and crewmember. A few feet distant a twenty-five-foot crater leaves evidence of the tragedy that changed Shanksville. A large cross was brought to the site. It was placed there by Somerset Christian Missionary Alliance Church.

The American and state flags wave over the fields where the Boeing 757 went down. The Flight 93 flag depicts the three sites where terror struck. It was designed by Gene Stilp of Harrisburg. The stripes represent the thirteen original colonies. The big "93" replaces the fifty stars and the wording tells us "Our Nation will remember and eternally honor the heroes of Flight 93." Benches at the site bear the names of the passengers and crewmembers. The boards were covered with artifacts left by visitors. The artifacts left at the site by thousands of visitors and mourners are periodically collected, preserved in the Somerset historical building and will be part of the permanent memorial.

A "Let's Roll" monument was sent from citizens in Colorado. It is dedicated to the first citizen heroes of the twenty-first century. Another "Let's Roll" monument was designed by Herbert Ermenger of Guatemala City, who sent two granite plaques. The second was larger than the first because he wanted to put more on it. He has a deep appreciation for our country. It was his way of saying thank you to the passengers and crew of Flight 93 and the American nation as well. The large one, weighing 450 pounds, arrived on time for the first anniversary. It was placed at the memorial site by county employees. Ermenger viewed the ceremony and his monument on CNN coverage of the anniversary.

The bronze plaque bearing the names of all thirty-three passengers and seven crewmembers was first displayed at the temporary memorial on Lambertsville Road in the weeks following the crash. It was affixed to a granite stone and dedicated on March 11, 2002. Family members of the heroes as well as folks from all over the country converged on Stonycreek Township to join in the prayers and activities at the site on Skyline Drive.

A little chapel has become a refurbished spiritual monument to the heroes of Flight 93. It offers comfort, reassurance and consolation to families of the victims and others who come to pay their respects. It had been an aged and secluded house of worship for nearly a century. The little white chapel was forever transformed when Flight 93 thundered across the serene, tranquil hills, shattering the silence of a peaceful morning. It forever transformed this site into holy ground.

The dragline remains where it was when the crash occurred, but strip mining is no longer done in this immediate area. An American flag was placed on top of the dragline to honor the amazing Americans who won the first fight against terrorism.

September 11, 2003, was a beautiful fall day much like the same date two years earlier. A beautiful evening sunset was streaming across the Laurel Highlands as the strains of our national anthem rose from this now historic hillside. A few moments later, with the Stars and Stripes held by a multitude of people, their voices blended in a prayer that rose far beyond the skies of this great nation as all sang "God Bless America."

SOMERSET COUNTY, PENNSYLVANIA

Shanksville is a friendly little hamlet of serene atmosphere and a peaceful environment.

The bridge is the gateway to Shanksville. The Stonycreek River flows beside the town.

This was once a thriving settlement of various businesses but today Ida's store has gained the status of the only store in town.

Shanksville

Terry Shaffer, fire chief, directs his firemen along the parade route on July 4, 2002. This was the contingent that responded initially to Flight 93. The Shanksville Fire and Police Departments were among the first on the scene.

The Camp Allegheny float is pulled by Dave Keppen on July 4, 2002. In patriotic colors the float represents the Ten Commandments. These carry a special message and are just as relevant as they always were.

The God Bless America Float is made up of children, parents and bales of hay from the surrounding fields. Carter and Shelby Slade are among the youngsters.

SOMERSET COUNTY, PENNSYLVANIA

Religion played an important role in the lives of Shanksville's settlers and again in the lives of current residents when their town was abruptly transformed by the events of September 11.

The living flag marches along Main Street before forming a human American flag on July 4, 2002.

A golden steel angel points toward the site of the Flight 93 tragedy.

Shanksville

As one approaches the site on Skyline Drive the memorial can be seen overlooking the crash site, which is several yards into the field and marked by a flag.

Stars were placed on the plywood board of the temporary memorial—one for each passenger and crewmember on Flight 93.

Above: A large wooden cross was placed at the site in October 2001.

Right: Father Adrian D. Tirpak, TOR, and his sister Connie Szmidt were visiting the temporary memorial when he met a good friend, Sister Mary DePaul Porta, RSM, who was also visiting.

Shelby, Andy, Carter and Dawson display their Fisher Price airplane symbolic of the Boeing 757 now embedded in a nearby field.

The many flags posted at the memorial site each have a story to tell.

Somerset County, Pennsylvania

Right: Slate freedom angels were placed at the site in December 2001. They were created by Tammy and Eric Peterson of Reading, Pennsylvania. Here Jayne Wagner, Shelby Slade, Leigh Snyder, Chuck Wagner and Lara Stutzman are surrounded by the angels. Christine Snyder (no relation to Leigh) perished in the crash. Leigh made connections with Christine's mother-in-law via e-mail. Here the Leigh Snyder and Wagner families and friends are decorating a slate angel for Christine's family, who live in Hawaii.

Below: A "Let's Roll" monument was sent from Colorado citizens. It is dedicated to the first citizen heroes of the twenty-first century.

Shanksville

The bronze plaque bearing the names of all thirty-three passengers and seven crewmembers was first displayed at the temporary memorial on Lambertsville Road.

This wreath is made up of pictures of all forty passengers, flight attendants and crewmembers who perished in the tragedy.

This "Let's Roll" plaque was designed by Herbert Ermenger of Guatemala City, who sent two granite plaques to show his appreciation and respect.

The Flight 93 flag, designed by Gene Stilp, is attached to the plywood board that carries the messages of many visitors.

The color guard marches to the memorial site where they gave a twenty-one-gun salute. Notice the numerous media in the background.

A little chapel located along the Stultzmantown Road in Shanksville affords solace, consolation, comfort and support to families of the victims as well as visitors to the site.

SOMERSET COUNTY, PENNSYLVANIA

Right: The dragline is an excavation machine that has been part of the landscape at the site since 1995. It was used for strip or surface mining. It is no longer in use, but now flies an American flag as a tribute.

Below: Among the many artifacts at the crash site, this stone best described the sentiments of many Americans.

Shanksville

Above: The students and staff of Shanksville-Stonycreek School District joined in a special project to spell out their sentiments. It was the idea of elementary teacher Karen Miller. Superintendent Gary A. Singel and J.P. O'Connor are on the roof checking out the lettering. Jim Will, a pilot, flew his little plane over the Shanksville school and captured the perfect formation.

Below: Old Glory marks the actual burial site—the sacred crater—the cemetery of the forty passengers and crewmembers who were aboard Flight 93. Citizens around the country joined in a prayerful spirit of patriotism. It was our affirmative answer to the words of Francis Scott Key: "Oh say does that Star Spangled Banner yet wave; O'er the land of the free and the home of the brave."

About the Author

Sister Anne Frances Pulling, RSM, MS, is a native of Long Island, New York, and a graduate of College Misericordia in Dallas, Pennsylvania, and Fordham University in New York City. Sister has taught in various schools in New York and Pennsylvania and been published in ten local pictorial history books.